# Without My Asking

# Without My Asking

## Asking

## Robert Cording

CAVANKERRY
PRESS

CavanKerry Press Ltd.
Fort Lee, New Jersey
www.cavankerrypress.org

Publisher's Cataloging-In-Publication Data
(Prepared by The Donohue Group, Inc.)
Names: Cording, Robert, author.
Title: Without my asking / Robert Cording.
Description: First edition. | Fort Lee, New Jersey : CavanKerry Press, 2019.
Identifiers: ISBN 9781933880747
Subjects: LCSH: Life—Poetry. | LCGFT: Poetry.
Classification: LCC PS3553.O6455 B64 2019 | DDC 811/.54—dc23

Book design and typesetting by Mayfly Design
First Edition 2019, Printed in the United States of America

NOTABLE VOICES
CavanKerry
PRESS

CavanKerry Press is proud to publish the works of
established poets of merit and distinction.

CavanKerry Press is grateful for the support it receives
from the New Jersey State Council on the Arts.

# Also by Robert Cording

**Poetry:**

*Life-list* (1987)
*What Binds Us to This World* (1991)
*Heavy Grace* (l996)
*Against Consolation* (2001)
*Common Life* (2006)
*Walking with Ruskin* (2010)
*A Word in My Mouth: Selected Spiritual Poems* (2013)
*Only So Far* (2015)

**Edited:**

*In My Life: Encounters with the Beatles* (1998)
(with Shelli Jankowski-Smith and E. J. Miller-Laino)

*for Colleen, now and always*

*(in memory of Muriel Norma Cording)*

The soul in paraphrase, heart in pilgrimage . . .

GEORGE HERBERT, "PRAYER (1)"


Teach us to number our days . . .

PSALM 90


"Yes . . ." that peculiar
affirmative. "Yes . . ."
A sharp, indrawn breath,
half groan, half acceptance,
that means "Life's like that.
We know *it* (also death)."

ELIZABETH BISHOP, "THE MOOSE"

# Contents

# Three.

# Four.

# Without My Asking

# Evening Prayer with Opening Question

What does it mean to call this life my own,
as if it could be possessed
                                      rather than simply lived,
its discrete stages just that,

even if, at moments,
                              they seemed intentional
(as though signs had been posted and were readable)?

A life to lose? Certainly.
                              To gain?—that, too, I suppose,
though my aim has been an I
          that would be worth giving away,

or back to you, Lord, whom I love
          but know almost wholly as a door
closed against my knocking,

                              the beat of my hands a song
I'd like to think I make with your silence,

a song that makes me who it is I am,
          but could more easily be failure's reoccurrence.

**One.**

# Cedar Waxwings

It might have been Euripides
or any one of those Greek playwrights
with their eyes focused on the tragic
who said, "No man can count on his happiness,"
which, while true, doesn't mean I should not
welcome this flock of cedar waxwings,
all silky brown, gray, and yellow,
gliding in like good luck.

They hop from branch to branch
in the hawthorn, the air enlivened
with their high, thin whistles, and bob
on the thinner branches of a chokecherry,
buoyant as they pick the red berries
and hold them momentarily in their beaks
or pass a berry from one bird to another—
and then, all at once, take flight.

# Talking Turkey

Eleven wild turkeys have walked out of the woods
into my backyard. *Turkey*: an English mistake,
probably due to homesickness, this New World
native looking something like a fowl
the first settlers had eaten back in England,
where its name named not the bird
but the trade route through Turkey
that delivered the birds to European markets.

#

Had the expression been available, Ben Franklin
might have said, in response to the country's
choice of a representative bird, let's "talk turkey."
He found the bald eagle of dubious moral character.
He probably saw that lazy bully swoop in
and plunder an osprey's fish. Wise old Ben knew
the bottom line with the bald eagle was profits,
whereas turkeys "come by their living honestly."

#

Outside my window, they go about their business.
They're congregating now for winter.
I remember a poet describing their loyalty
to one another: a hen in a topmost branch
flapping its wings to shake down apples
for the commonwealth of others waiting below.
Intelligent in the wild, they are not the "turkey"
we domesticated into stupidity over time.

#

I've placed a print of Audubon's wild turkey
on my study wall: a male looking over
its shoulder, as in a portrait of a founding father.
Audubon catches both his weathered,
no-nonsense attitude and the plump plain beauty
of browns, creams, and bronze-green iridescence.
Grounded, down-to-earth, the turkey
seems to know exactly who he is.

#

Hunted almost to extinction, domesticated,
then reintroduced into the wild so we could hunt
them again—I'm thankful for their comeback.
And thankful for what passes as their casual pardon
as they go about their work, flourishing
at the edges we've left them. Right now,
they're scraping the fallen leaves with their feet
for the bounty of red and white oak nuts.

#

And I'm especially thankful for the way
this no fanfare bird has given transport:
one evening, crossing over the crest
of a hill, I saw a rafter of turkeys
sitting in the topmost branches of an old oak
like people in the upper windows of a house,
their quiet, thoughtful bodies silhouetted
against a full moon roosting in the tree with them.

# Supermoon

"The heavens," our weather-person said,
"would be putting on quite a show."

And, when the perigee full moon,
the earth, and sun lined up, the moon

slowly reddened, then went dark
as the earth mantled it. It felt as if

the moon was melting away
or as if some magician god was pulling

a sheer black cloth over
the moon's naked shoulders and hips.

#

Moths ticked against the glass of a window,
trying to reach a light left on upstairs.

In the bog behind our house, stands of trees
darkened into shades packed tight in a boat

crossing into the underworld. And the moon's
dark hole became the lens of a telescope

through which we saw the stars, and the galaxy
the stars belonged to, and then, against our will,

the galaxies beyond our galaxy, the dizzying
sensation of space opening on space.

#

Afterwards, when we tried to translate
what we had felt, words were no help.

In bed, unable to sleep, we watched highlights
of the eclipse on the Weather Channel,

wanting to feel again how we had been changed.
And after that—still restless, we turned

in the dark from side to side, into and out of
the silvery light that transformed the larches

outside our windows into fantastical forms.

# Middle Tint

I'm standing in my front yard
trying hard to see like a painter,
my raised hands framing the imagined
canvas: *Barn, Field, Afternoon Sun, and Larches.*

I've been thinking about Ruskin again.
More than half my life ago, I read
straight through *Modern Painters.*
When it came to landscapes, Ruskin said

the truly skilled painter devoted himself
to the *middle tint*, those humble gradations
of browns, grays, and greens
that provide a kind of ground

for nature's isolated extremes
of shade and sheen. So I'm studying
that palette—the barn's
muted browns, and the heat-dulled

yellowy-green field that finds
its complements in a green-gold stand
of larches and the five shades
of gray in the nearby stone walls.

But where the late afternoon sun
catches fire in the mid-branches
of one larch, I'm taken with those
flamboyant chiaroscuro touches

Ruskin warned against, and I want
to look beyond those duller colors

towards that deeply shaded,
but sun-shocked spot of revelation.

I suspect Ruskin feared how the ego cavorts,
turning everything it sees into its own
needy masquerade—not the world as it is,
but the enthrallments of the eye's

idealizations—and so tried to make
a sacrament of the middle tint
to hold in check his darkest compulsions.
Middle tint: like the church year's faithful

stretch of Ordinary Time,
or Ruskin's days of exacting observations,
the long tedium of attending to
the precise colors of a kingfisher's

secondaries, or the truth of water
the kingfisher hovers above,
a surface that can be seen
or seen through, but never both at once.

# Prayer While Driving Home
# After My Yearly Physical

Sixty-six, my shoulders rounded, my arches flattening, I am,
Lord, a small man, now a full inch shorter,
I'm told, than I once was. And so I pray

that my end-of-life diminishment might prove the occasion
for some late opening of my cramped borders,
this no-exit, small country of the self.

Lord, what I wouldn't give for a lifting up,
to be free of this strange human gift of making
something less out of something,

each day stunting the fresh opportunity
to become Blake's towering giant,
the four-fold angelic power you wanted us to be,

if only we didn't make ourselves
tiny with our incessant self-interest, our hearts
clamped around our enemies,

our narrow sympathies, and unrelenting prideful gloom.
Lord, at every moment I have been a beginner,
lost in the bewildering wilderness of my ignorance.

Now that I am smaller, I pray that it will be
easier to recede from the center of my picture
and find this unexpected reprieve from vanity.

Let everything around me grow taller, Lord,
and more vivid, newly made, like these autumn maples
coloring the air, or this roadside red-tailed hawk,

its wingspan blinding as it crosses my windshield,
the road for a moment dark, then bright,
bearing me on, a small man nearing his exit.

# Dock Life

Late Tuesday afternoon in late October
and the dock where I sat this morning
in a wool shirt is now all sun
rubbing the surfaces of old wood into a patina
of amber warmth. The lake turns
summer's blue again and the few boats
not yet taken out of the water scissor up
and down our small bay. A heron flies by,
each wing-beat visible, as if it were flying
in slow motion and had time to waste.
Like me, I guess. Recently retired, I've got
whole days to try and let go of the person
I've been so the person I don't yet know
can introduce himself.

Now three arriving boats group
and drop anchor in the leisurely amplitude
of afternoon sun. Six teenage boys,
just let out of school, turn up
Springsteen's "Having a Party,"
then strip and dive into the lake,
their unabashed screams echoing as they hit
the cold water. It could be July
except for those screams and how quickly
they're back on the boat, wrapping
themselves in towels and sweatshirts.
And already the unearthly earthly light
that had burnished the docks and houses
and fastened down for a few hours,
is floating away on the half-light
of dusk, one moment arriving, another

departing as if time were speeding up
and entering my body as I sit here.

I've heard the Dalai Lama visualizes
his death every day. I can only vaguely
imagine what's still to come. On the far side
of the lake, a few house lights flicker on.
In another, a television's blue comfort.
Two of the boats have gone off. It's just me,
marooned on my dock, and one teenager
reluctant to move on, listening to music
and holding his face to the sun on this still lit
eastern side. And a merganser that,
brought here by the rhythms of migration,
and swimming in slow, casual circles,
its reddish head a glowing point of last light,
seems almost too perfectly at ease.

# November

No order, not even chronology, to these snippets
of spliced-together home movies, digitalized

by a niece and arriving in the mail today—a flash drive
of my life over fifty years ago.

October lingered on and on, then ended.
I've spent this first November afternoon, cold rain

darkening the slate of the patio,
and now the day darkening in the windows,

watching my grandparents and parents walk toward me,
or more accurately, toward the camera, images

of Christmas and Easter, birthday parties and anniversaries,
tables piled high with turkeys and roast beef,

with trays of cold cuts and potato and noodle salads,
with Seagram's 7, Jack Daniel's, and Johnnie Walker.

Everyone dancing and eating. How different and similar
they look. Their feelings are commonplace and profound,

and, of course, unknowable. Such pleasure now to find
my ten-year-old self diving off the dock in unison

with my brothers, and then, as we loved to see
when we were children, flying up out of the water in reverse,

returned once again to the dock in a kind of comic eternity.
There's also the sad undertow of the dead—

grandparents, parents, aunts, uncles, cousins—
even if they are almost a story now, their lives

ordered in retrospect, made complete.
All afternoon, the negotiations of memory

have worked out its algorithms of happiness and pain,
figuring forth the sound of Uncle Bill's laugh,

and my brothers' accordions and the clacking shoes
of my mother and her mother, dancing polkas

then holding their weak hearts, out of breath, wheezing
and laughing. Then the other side of the ratio—

the morphine cloud of my dying mother,
my father's blind-gray eye and then the coma

and the ghost-touch of his hand days before he died.
Here, the ghost in the screen is me, intent

on putting into words what's already long gone.
When I look out the window, the avenues between the trees

are clear and deep, a somber vocabulary of gray and brown.
I should take a walk, but I turn back to my grandfather

fishing in this digital after-life, towels drying in the sun
at Montauk, then my father brushing snow off

our finned Ford Fairlane. Then he's behind the wheel,
saying, in the secondhand of memory, "Power of Power,"

as he presses down on the accelerator and the Ford's V-8
lurches forward and my brothers and I feel the thrill

of all that horsepower, our bodies driven back into the seats,
and then my mother is admonishing him, telling him

to slow down and he does, and my brothers groan,
the thrill over almost as soon as it began.

# Obituary

In your obituary I concluded, "Muriel lives on in . . . "
and went on to name myself, my two brothers,
and your eleven grandchildren. I may have been thinking
of Pasternak who said something like our life
in others is our immortality, or I may have just been
looking for a way to make your life continue
even as I announced that it was already finished.
Well, Mother, I confess, if your life continued
in mine, I have been wasting it. I've forgotten
what you taught me: how, despite whatever may be
happening, one gets up and gets going.
Cook something. Do the dishes. Take a walk
to the pond. Clean your closet. Fix the faucet.
You never suggested or asked. You ordered.
Once, on a late Sunday afternoon, the dread
of school overtaking my childhood self, I was
lying around on the living room rug, like the sullen
lodged in the mud of Dante's Inferno, complaining
about how I was bored, bored, bored,
when you slapped me, and told me to get my coat
and go outside. Late autumn, the trees empty
of leaves, everything brown and gray, I gathered
a pail full of fallen crabapples—the task you'd given
me to complete—then began to throw them hard
at the trunks of trees in the adjacent empty lot,
loving the pulpy thwack and the way those apples
that struck home left a dripping mark. I didn't want
to stop. I was punishing those trees the way you had
punished me, but soon I wasn't thinking anything
at all. I was breathing fast, and I was sitting
on the cold ground, and the pail was empty,

and I was hearing the silence that comes after,
and I swear, I could feel the pinks and grays
of the sky inside my body, but that must have had
more to do with what I'd done, which was hardly anything
more than complete a simple task, like this poem,
Mother, which I've ordered myself to write
because I didn't know what else to do.

# Poverty

So much sitting still these past months, hoarding
my sorrows, looking out at another day's news-
paper being buried by the accumulating snow,

my daily sighs a kind of catch-all for the poverty
of everything I need to speak. You are dead,
my words cannot alter that. And here I am,

your oldest son, addressing *you,* as if
you might answer back, the way you told me
your dead husband, my father, spoke with you.

I keep circling our last weeks together,
those days of disappearing hours, of grinding bones,
of wetting and soiling yourself, of pills

and incomprehension, the drugged sun rising
and setting, the palm trees waving
their venetian blind shadows across the grass.

I have felt so often these past two months
as if something immense and absolute had entered
my life and gone away, and nothing had come clear.

Last night, calling my dog, I saw myself wander
to the edge of the electric fence and bark into
the darkness at something I couldn't see, but felt was there.

#

Nights were always worse. In the light you slept;
in the dark you needed to stay awake. Hour
after hour, you repeated, *I do and I don't,* as if that

equivocating mantra could help you arrive
at a final destination. Once you asked me to come close.
You whispered to me, "Do you know what's happening?"

Without tears, as tenderly and straightforwardly
as I could muster an answer, I said,
"You're dying, Mom." You slapped my arm hard,

and asked, "Why would you say such a thing?"
Neither one of us had a clue. I thought you knew.
*Dying*. Part of a language you'd spoken all your life

and yet inexact now, too definitive for
the decision you believed you were still making.
After that moment's question and answer,

your eyes widened and did not shut for two days.
Outside, the lake went on changing to no end
in the breeze. Friends came and went. You remained

fastened on the blank wall just above your bookcase
as if something was there none of us could see.
I thought you might have been waiting for my father

to come through, but when at last you spoke,
you cried out, "Abby, Abby, Abby," a childhood friend,
nothing that made sense at the moment, but who,

it turned out, was also dying a thousand miles away.

                #

It is my second Sunday with you. I am looking
out at the lake you loved from your double-wide,
watching a heron's slow glide from one side

of the lake to the other, and the stillness
just after it passes. I am recording this moment
as if it had something to say that I cannot say,

but it is only a record of a moment just before
your friends stopped by after church and the minister
gave you communion, the body of Christ dipped in

his blood, and pinned to your forehead
because you could not eat, your swallowing reflex
gone by now. In your clean, blue nightgown you are—

how do I say this without sounding unbelievable?—
radiant, propped up with pillows like a child
perched on that hospital bed in your living room

singing, or trying to, using up what would be the last
of your words on "In the Garden," hoping to hear
the one always calling through our voices of woe.

#

"What's happening outside?" you asked each day
when you still could talk, demanding a description
of the weather and what I saw out by the lake,

as if, your own present used up, you could still
have mine. I was happy to give it to you,
the live oak quivering with starlings, the palm

we planted for your 60th wedding anniversary
chattering in the breeze. You smiled and drifted away,
as if what I said only opened the ever-widening distance

between us, that sense that every bird,
every description of the sun on the lake water,
between clouds, or the scrim of rain moving in,

made you feel isolated, immune
to the contagious joy going on just outside
your door that you had always found so easily.

#

Near the end, you looked stunned, like someone
who knew help wasn't coming. You moaned,
and shook your head violently as if to ask,

"Why are you doing this to me?"
Then everything was groans and silence.
Neither of us could cross that baffling silence

even though I suspect that you felt as I did
that there was still so much to say.
Can we ever know who our parents are?

In your restless sleep you made sounds, a kind
of ur-language, or the language of children
before they are given to words. Some days

I tried to believe it was the language of the world
speaking beyond our human words. I knew
it was the language of the drugs I gave you.

And knew there was no knowing, nothing left
for me to do but sacrifice any thought
that I could make sense of what was now

arriving at its forgone, frayed conclusion.

#

Even so, I missed the moment of your death.
I'd been listening to the time between your breaths,
the intervals of not breathing longer and longer.

But when my wife whispered that you'd stopped
breathing, I was somewhere else, wondering if,
once the obligations of being who you were

were removed, your life's restlessness would finally end.
And this, which I need to say: that even then,
with death happening, it was impossible

to imagine your not being here. Yes, you are dead.
And I am trying still to find a vocabulary for
the half-glimpsed, half-recognized: who you were

and who it is I am because of you.
Your death's become a blank page I have to keep
writing on, my action as involuntary as my dog

barking into the darkness, as if, in doing so,
I could cross the silence of your disappearance,
or somehow keep your life from becoming smaller

and smaller, flattened even now in these pages.

# Little Did I Know

Not some underworld, just a dirt basement,
the February sun blinking out,
and not Orpheus, but Glenn,
my neighbor, friend, and also a plumber,
who belts out "Your Cheatin' Heart"
below me as he works on my cold oil burner.
His singing voice—a deep baritone
that belies his slight, wiry body and which
I have never heard or even suspected in the twenty years
I've known him—rises up through the floorboards
to where I am sitting wrapped in a blanket.
It's like suddenly waking up in my own house
to some sound I've never heard before,
but already feels familiar, like this old hymn,
"Old Rugged Cross," coming out of Glenn's mouth
and into my ears along with the sound
of the oil burner clicking on and then heat ticking
in the radiators.

            And now Glenn climbs
the stairs, his singing voice getting louder;
he pauses at the basement door to knock the dirt
from his shoes and pants, and here he is,
divorced for seven years, but bringing with him
a story about his new girlfriend,
and how even he can't believe his good luck;
he hasn't sung for God knows how long,
but now sings, he says, karaoke at the local bar
and in the choir at church. And then
he's out the door, singing "Crazy,"
his lungs working like bellows—and crazy
this man in the middle of his life

who I am just discovering knows how to sing,
his song still spilling warmly
in that good strong voice from his truck windows,
wide open in late winter.

**Two.**

# Roadside Petition After March Snow Melt

Will-less, their future a fait accompli,
they comically consecrate the road's still grassless lip

where they lie here and there
among the little green flames of skunk cabbage

lined up like votive candles. They could be
parables of lost sheep no one ever cared to look for—

this sweatshirt and sock, this one
red high-heeled shoe, this rusted harmonica, and what

must have been a love letter, now nearly wordless,
winter's ink bled out. And here's

a Spider-Man action figure with movable arms.
Lost and forgotten. Do you know

each of their stories, Lord,
or is our sad story always the same?

If I stand Spider-Man on his own two feet,
digging them into the sodden earth, then raise

his two arms in petition, will you hear our prayer:
*Lord, help us to be done with our grieving.*

# Overtaken

Always the same. Always new.
That throated trill, the throb of it

heard through shut windows
and doors, their inch-long bodies

inching in more and more March
light, the trees still in-waiting.

That first stirring, then frenzy—
peepers, coming alive with water

that slakes the dry thirst
of winter above and below ground

and a newborn sun's command
to begin again, begin again.

That wonder at what is going on.
And when I open the door,

the still cold air thrilling to this
riot of need, my entire body

turns inside out, and yields
to these spring passions of earth.

# Weather Report to My Mother

If you were alive, you'd have called
on the phone from Florida, asking
if it snowed, and how much. And, yes,
April arrived with its usual Fools' joke,
and I woke this northern morning to snow,
five inches or so, that seamlessly made
everything new, even the French doors
in the kitchen a trellis of blooming light.
My backyard gave me the new Jerusalem
in a vision as real as snow could make it.
That was hours ago, and now,
the low ceiling of clouds raised, the higher
spring sun bearing down, the snow
is already porous, riddled with holes,
water gurgling in miniature rivers or pooling,
and the roof's drip-line tap-tap-taps
a code on the hedges below. At my desk,
I'm doing my best to decipher it, but all
I've come up with is something you said
about the changeableness of the weather:
*life requires constant adjustments of hope.*
So now that my new Jerusalem's become
some last confection of winter,
I will report that what's here and now
is a small flock of dirt-loving juncos poking
for seeds where grass has been uncovered
by the coming-into-its-own April sun.

# Aubade

Here I am, waking in my old body again,
light on the wide pine boards, light mixed
with rain, the smell of April's softening dirt
rising up to our windows. You are sleeping,
the imprint of where my hand just held you
already disappearing. Last night still burns
with a low flame, our bodies younger
in my morning's memory, still freed,
if only temporarily, of their end-of-day rigidity,
more flexible and lithe, less paunchy even.
These days, our hunger appeasable,
the commotion of desire is less operatic,
both a way of asserting we're here and a way
of forgetting what we know too well—
our days are numbered. Now, no need
for Donne's tough talk that sent the sun packing;
it brings only this morning's light rain
and our grateful unimportant happiness,
the soon-to-come breakfast talk about the children—
who will come this weekend, who won't—
or the day's down-to-earth light, and whether
or not, later today, the sky will open up.

# Backyard Kingdom

*All the way to heaven is heaven,*
St. Catherine of Siena supposedly said,
and on most days, replete with
the stabbed, shot, run-over or into,
the stroked, heart-seized, and cancer-stricken,
I'd say bullshit and be done with it.

But today, at the tail-end of April, the sun warming
things up, I'm in shorts and a T-shirt, airing
my body out in a backyard chaise,
ready to emerge at last from winter's
long gestation in flannel and sweaters.
I'm listening to the nearby maple scratch an itch
against the clapboards,
and a downy woodpecker's got my foot tapping;
I'm letting things go, deep breathing
with a phoebe's wheezy *fee-be.*

Game on now, chickadees
have changed their tune—
it's all *hey sweetie, hey sweetie*
in the shine and sheen of new leaves.
A cardinal cranks up its engine, a catbird mews
and whistles, and a mourning dove responds
to the earth's tilt with soft, insistent coos.
When I shut my eyes, the wind DJs a mix
of all these singular voices, and the delirium
of their song won't take no for an answer.

*Take joy whenever you can get it,*
a wise old poet wrote and how can I refuse
this day that seems shaped for my delight,

this luck-of-the-draw moment in the sun,
the air rippling with a green iridescence.
So I say *I do, I do* to the day's proposal
and let myself float on April's soft warm air,
even my sweat-stained T-shirt like raiment,
for now my listening body an ear that hears
the kingdom always here.

# Prayer with Dog and Rooster

Lord, my golden is looking up at me
with those great big dog eyes of need,
and I am looking up at the bluing sky
as if you were there, and here I am,
at it again, gazing out my windows
full of pent-up praise and soft-headed hopes.
I swear getting closer to you should come
with instructions, or one of those *Guides*
*for Dummies*, a thought that reminds me
of my fears of being only what I am,
an old professor who's read too many
spiritual books. It's early, Lord, the rising sun
fitting itself into my window,
and my neighbor's rooster has crowed
a dozen times already, and I'm up, reading
psalms, ready as ever for something
to happen, though I suspect I'm praying
as if I could make you into something solid,
a table, say, where I could sit and eat.
If nothing else, I suppose my humorous crusade
has given you a laugh or two. So I'll keep
at it, breathing in, breathing out, believing
as always that just outside my window
there's a vision to be had or not had,
as with every moment, the rooster calling
the day to my attention if nothing else.

# Spring Again

It was a time of contradictions.
His great fatigue, spring's great energies.

He looked out from inside his head.
The sun flashed in rivers and lakes.

Forsythia brightened winter's end.
Magnolias blossomed extravagantly.

Everything he said, he repeated, like a prayer.
His scroll of enigmatic texts read like his own scriptures.

Then cherry trees pushed out their little pink flowers.
Birds nattered on and on about desire.

Spring again, and its freight of childlike promises.
It exhausted him. None of them did him any good.

Back home after his funeral, we want to feel.
We don't want to feel. Days of moods

and half-moods that never reveal themselves.
Of thoughts that refuse to take shape.

A robin hops from branch to branch.
Shakes a burst of rain from the leaves.

Our eyes can't help discovering May's new greens.
It seems wrong not to love the yellow tulips.

We do not know if his prayers were answered or not.
We have his texts, which we cannot read.

# Sugar Maple

I like to stand under it, and look up,
through the small clearings between branches,

their rims of green leaves focusing the blue
of the sky as if I am looking into some past.

Planted in the forties after the war,
this tree grew with the children of the woman

who lived in this house. Truth is, I hardly knew her.
I know from her son she's living in a nursing home.

She doesn't remember the names of her children
carved in the maple.

I've read that Alzheimer's patients can look at trees
so attentively they enter a Zen-like state of meditation.

I want to believe it's so,
as I want to believe in what I have felt

more than once—that this maple was saying something
I had to hear, to decipher, and write down.

Something recognizable, but withheld,
wordless, something

I was certain I knew—as the woman who lived here knew
this sugar maple and the way it holds June's long light

in its canopy, or even now might know
her children's names, even if she can no longer call them in

or put them into the words of her knowing.

# Spring Begetting

My one-year-old grandson John has climbed up
on the couch where I have been reading Updike,
and, standing, looks out the window to the lilacs
where a catbird spills itself in long bursts
of *toowees, cluks, whooits,* and *meows* and now
he, too, finds his way to runs of throaty vowels
and a comedic tumble of consonants that possess
the force and urgency of a sentence revving up
against the impossibility of catching all it hopes
to describe, this little window world pollen-heavy,
my grandson's buzzing wordlike sounds working
like bees to gather in spring's excess.

And now rain is falling through the sunlight,
the newly green lilac leaves glistening,
and John has tottered off towards the sounds
of our dog in the kitchen; I am returning slowly
to Updike, the sound of his sentences mixing
with the catbird who is at it again, the two of them
full of a sexual longing for the completion of form.
I hear him again—not the preening Updike,
chest fluffed out in display, but the man
who believed, *the world is the host; it must be
chewed,* tasted in the sweet pouring forth of words.

# Source

An hour before sunset and that golden light
stretching the days of mid-June illuminates
our bedroom in the light of religious paintings
when something is revealed. I'm lying on our bed,
reading a poet I like who keeps jabbing
at people's sentimental "love
for everyday things"—roadside flowers, sparrows,
a sugar bowl and spoon—that cannot save us
from the "void ahead." I laugh,
but then start thinking how, only a few minutes
ago, I looked up and saw you disappearing
around the edge of the shower curtain.
So, I'm revealing the source of my happiness—
your nearly sixty-year-old still lovely ass.
I might have shouted out a Hallelujah,
unbidden praise, except I was afraid
you'd startle and slip. But there it was,
mooning me as Yahweh mooned Moses,
showing him the hind parts, that fraction
of the whole, before vanishing again into mystery,
or, just then, a cleft in the rocks. You will resist
the analogy, no doubt, yet what I know
of Yahweh is just as blank and, truly, as loved;
I learned in Sunday school to love
what we never see by loving what we do—
this plum-colored mug, say, underglazed
in deep blue we brought back from Cornwall.
Bedside, it's giving off steaming auras of tea
and waiting for you to step from behind the curtain
as this golden light yields to the loosening dark
and, ultimately, to that emptiness
we can never see into that waits beyond
the little, loved kingdom of our everyday things.

**Three.**

# Soleil & Sons

I have been reading your better servant
George Herbert again, and I'm trying to turn
my day into prayer, praying as the toast rises
with the toaster's tinny bell and the tea leaves
turn water into English Breakfast tea,
and praying as I slice strawberries and add
their redness to a bowl of granola.
I'm grateful this morning for this cinnamon toast
and for the local baker who made it, and for
the French word for sun and the punning name
of the bakery, and for the sun that arrived
this morning without my asking.
Soleil & Sons, Soleil & Sons, Soleil & Sons,
why not add those words to my prayer,
the glass of my watch making a small sun
of the actual sun that forks and darts
along the walls and across the ceiling, multiplying
like those five loaves, like sun and sons.
Maybe this is how Herbert's prayer became an elixir
that kept gratitude in mind even when it didn't,
that carried the whole, given ordinary day
inside it, his entire body feeling
as if it could break into applause for nothing
more than the floor he swept clean *for thy sake*,
nothing explaining the way love took hold.

# Looking Up in the Backyard

Lowering the paper, I look up at the news
the wind's brought to my dog. It's the fox
that appears in the field from time to time,
and, foxlike, seems to know the invisible line
of the electric fence my dog won't cross.

My golden retriever runs to that line, stops,
and barks, and will not stop barking
when the fox lies itself down in the sun,
its red fur setting fire to the grass, and looks
at both of us from the solitude of being itself,

nothing human in its makeup. My dog,
halfway between the fox and myself,
seems pissed off at the fox's wildness,
or the slow twitching of its tail, or maybe
at not being able to reach beyond her reach.

Something about this scene gets me
remembering those ancient tales in which
birds and animals became human, and humans
birds and animals, the transformations
quick and fluid, the blue heron folding

its wings into a fisherman casting into
the clear stream winding through a meadow.
Now my dog is acting just like me:
she seems to recognize the huge gap between
what might happen and what will happen,

and she's trotting back to the house
where there's a dish of food and a bowl
of water and someone who will pet her
before he turns back to the newspaper,
missing the fox rise and disappear into trees.

# My Neighbor's Mailbox

is the usual silver color, oversized
*Wonder Bread* shape on which he's stenciled
"Welcome Family and Friends."
My neighbor and I are friendly.
I appreciate the way he's often tuning up
an engine or working around his yard.
We talk about the weather, or how our houses
are always in need of more attention
than we can give them. Last week
he told me of a robbery only three doors away
from where we stood, and the loaded gun
he keeps in his closet. He wondered
about our neighbor with the half-shaved head
and face full of piercings and tattoos.
I was looking at his mailbox
and thinking about how hard it is
to extend an idea of love into the actual world
and have it apply to more than the people
just like yourself. In that world my neighbor's hours
at work have been cut back. Lately, when
walking past his house, I've found him
just standing aimlessly in his driveway.
My grandfather would have called my neighbor
a good, hard-working man. My neighbor
likes to call me *The Professor* and ask me
if I'm on another sabbatical when I walk by,
the joke, as we both know too well,
an acknowledgment of another kind of difference.
He might be surprised to know how we're alike,
how, despite my professed, but mostly imagined,
good-willed attempts to love all my neighbors,

I'm all too wary of anyone who drives past
me on my walks and doesn't wave,
or worse, comes to the door just about everyone
who knows me knows we never use,
and waits on the other side to be welcomed.

# Across the Water

First, wind dying off with a kind of shudder,
dock flags dropping limply against their poles;
then the dark spools in like fog, the evening
quiet enough to hear a man's voice traveling
from somewhere in the middle of the lake
to where I'm sitting on the shore—*Why?*

A woman replies, *There is no reason.*
I see the dark outline of a canoe emerging,
and hear the paddles' lift and return to water.
*Did I do something wrong?*—it's the man,
his voice like someone being punished
for something he does not remember having done.

The moon rises above the dull blade
of the mountains. *It's not anything
that can be explained,* she says, then, *what can be said?*
I know how both of them want to speak, yet know
nothing can be said to rectify what is happening,
each word a fishbone caught in their throats.

And after they paddle back into the darkness,
the lake water lapping against the canoe,
then against the shore, the night reseals itself
as if there had never been a canoe
or those voices' doomed history, but only this
story I recognize as my own, long ago.

# Lake George

*(July 4th, 2014)*

The air cool and fresh, the lake's a dazzle of
whitecaps and gray-blue waves, the sun
breaking out in applause between a rhapsody
of wind-driven cumulus. Flags snap
on decks and boathouses and fly straight out
on the boats that skip up and down the lake.

I've put down the newspaper's infernal sadness,
and I'm enjoying a group of teenagers trying to tie
two of those rented pontoon boats together.
They're already half-drunk, laughing, happy
in their incompetency, a Marx Brothers' movie
of a rope thrown from one boat to the other.

In the foreground, a trio of kayaks, red, yellow,
and blue, and the glint of paddles making
figure eights in air and water. A backdrop
of mountains looks down like gods who have
seen it all a million times, but, stretched out
in the sun, are as yet too lazy to exert their whimsy.

In their shade, five seemingly still sailboats, give
the speedboats their speed; their distant sails tilt
white triangles into the wind as in a child's drawing.
The *Minne-Ha-Ha* steams down the far side
of the lake and the *Lac du Saint Sacrement* huffs
and puffs up this side, each of them packed tight

with people reveling in the mindless freedom
of a perfect day off, waving to all of us on our docks,
as the two boats blow greetings to one another.

Everything shimmers in the sun, and I'm imagining
the whole scene as one of those Impressionist paintings,
a beach scene of people dressed in gay colors

and holding color-coordinated umbrellas, happy to be
exactly where they are, or so it always seems.
And since I'm looking again at the ongoing comedy
on those pontoon boats, I might as well prescribe
a dose of that teenage idea of freedom without obligation
for myself and forget about finding some meaning

I'd only force on this rapturous day anyhow—
I'll just sip my gin and tonic, and enjoy
my unpursued happiness on this freighted day.

# Room with Three Windows

August. Only the immediate is apparent.
Lilac leaves, rhododendrons, holly,
trunk and branches of an ash. Everything so near,
pressing up to the screens. A kind of otherness
in the ordinary catbird's dark eye
in the window. In the elegant precision of a wren.

The hours are clocked by the leaves' green
changing in the light. Silver green. Bright green.
Dusky gold-green. What comes and goes,
comes and goes unrehearsed. So little happens.
So much. Day after day, arriving
at the windows: what is new, then old, then new.

# Plenty

*(Audubon Center, Santa Fe, New Mexico)*

We are eating breakfast in the green shade
of the tallest cottonwoods. The sun is coming
into its own now, the grasses have dried,
and there's the smell of sage and earth warming
in the light. An orchard of apricot,
apple and pear trees surrounds us,
and a docent is hanging just-filled feeders,
which look like giant red bell-shaped flowers
with yellow centers, for the hummingbirds.
We do not have to wait long before the air
is busy with their fervor. When we name them—
Black-chinned, Broad-tailed, Rufous, Calliope—
it feels as if we see them more clearly
and intimately, their gorgets glowing purple
and black, rose, and copper, their buzzing
wings beating with different vibratos.
They are zipping behind us and in front of us,
coming to a standstill next to our ears
or right before our eyes, this excess of color
and sound filling the air for us,
as if our sole purpose is simply to take pleasure
in the day's clean heat, in the hummingbirds
renewing themselves at the feeders,
in our easy passage into this plenty.

# Remembering Debbie in Chimayo

A name I'd almost forgotten, but here it is—
*Debbie,* with a little soap bubble heart over the i—
written on one of the photographs
of the dead or suffering who are elevated by love
and tacked on these church walls.
Of course it's a different Debbie
than the one who took care of my mother.
Ex-drug addict, born-again Lutheran,
once engaged to an alcoholic who died
and left her a yellow muscle car,
Debbie, who mowed the church lawn
to get by, and smiled through the cancer
that took her own life six months
after my mother's death.

Near the dirt pilgrims come for,
a little plastic orange scoop waits hopefully
to be lifted up. There is no grief
that has not been cried here,
no hope left unhoped for a better life
for the unlucky. In this place of holy kitsch,
its walls covered with photographs,
with crosses made of hair, mosaics, wood,
its every available resting place
crammed with flowers, mostly plastic, and stones
Sharpied with messages for the dead,
I remember how Debbie once told me
she loved to mow during a sun shower,
all the colors of the sun coming out
while it rained, and then the parking lot steaming
after the sun returned.

It's raining here, hard, the sound
of God's footsteps striding across the roof—
something Debbie liked to say.
Kneeling in this church to consecrate the suffering
that can never be understood,
my prayer turns into another memory
of Debbie, tired and in pain from her cancer,
sitting with my mother, side by side,
in the brown and blue La-Z-Boy recliners,
near the end of my mother's life. The two of them
are holding hands, and talking away the afternoon
until they pause, feeling the touch
of afternoon sunlight on their skin
as it passes through the darkened living room.
Then Debbie gets up to leave, but stops
in the doorway, the canted sun behind her.
She is saying *goodbye,* but my mother insists
that she say, *see you*, never *goodbye,*
as if there were always some hope
in the yet to come; or at least in the moment,
each of them seeing and seen by the other.

# Roadside Homily

Blessed are these vultures, robed in black,
blood on their beaks, on their clawed toes,
who attend most single-mindedly
to what we most want to forget—death
we rush past at highway's edge,
today a belly-opened, fly-ridden fawn
around which they shuffle deliberately,
wings jutting disjointedly.

                    The vultures say
everything is flesh, nothing more. Blessed
is the kingdom where all things end
to clear the way once more for beginnings.
For theirs is the kingdom of transfiguration,
of the forever stilled taken piece by piece
into their ungainly bodies and, later, lifted up,
their outstretched wings translating
the afternoon's warm, rising thermals
in elegant, widening circles.

# Toast to My Dead Parents

My parents worshipped at the altar
of the present, each moment
an opportunity for bickering,
for one of them, in their elaborate game
of cat-and-mouse—*Didn't you say*
*it was going to rain today?*
*Who put the salt and pepper here,*
*it's gone in the cabinet above the stove*
*for sixty years*—to gain a slight advantage.

They were entertaining, their fights
like tickets to the Amusement Park
we could never afford.
My father, who liked word play,
said they were keeping things *fresh.*
They said good morning
in myriad phrases—*the eggs are dry,*
*you burnt the English muffin again,*
*where did you put my pills?*
That got the morning going like the cuckoo
popping out of the Black Forest
kitchen clock to jeeringly announce
the hour that was an hour too late,
each blaming the other for oversleeping.

It was, I guess, in its sad, crazy
destructive way, a form of communication.
My brothers and I never understood
their day-long bickering, nor that
nagging devotion to each other,
one of them unfailingly present
at the other's bedside in sickness.

They never complained about money,
lived happily by the house rule of *enough,*
as in whatever we have is enough,
yet seemed always to be in need
of something that wasn't to be had—
something intangible they wanted
to hold with their hands, or be
able to say with the fluency of words
which never came, or came
garbled and incompletely, or twisted
whatever they were looking for
into another insult.

Their bickering grew less playful,
more cat batting a half-dead mouse
back and forth between its paws,
as they tried to ward off
the clock-tick of dying's boredom.
They certainly kept things *fresh,*
the freedom of destruction, I guess,
better than some quiet descent
into death. And so, dear parents, I toast you,
toast all those words volleyed back and forth,
the two of you filled with some great need
that could never be fully met,
true believers in all that might be
that never was, hopeless
romantics to the bitter end.

# Morning Prayer with Hopkins' Kestrel

*It is required you do awake your faith,*
Paulina says to Leontes, and these crows,
spurting from the night's silence into the gray before
dawn's rose, yell it in through my open window.

I am slow to cooperate. O Lord, I owe you
at least the modest diligence of looking carefully
each day; so let my narcoleptic steps deliver me outside,
the sky blueing this day at the tail end of summer.

Here is my morning report. High clouds.
An intermittent breeze, two boxy cedars bowing stiffly,
a frenzied swarm of gnats forming and re-forming
earthbound clouds in the shade of the barn.

A slight reddening in the apples. The grass stands
straight up, full of last night's rain. Two nuthatches
spiral an ash trunk, probing. A squirrel rides the wave
of a branch until it stills. Towhees call out their names,

and the flare of a cardinal streaks into a nearby maple,
the red confection of its crown laughably exotic.
A hummingbird levitates, darts forward into the yellow
cave of a daylily, then returns to the light.

The sun has concentrated itself in a silver bowl of water
I've put out for the dog. Yes, another list, Lord. Call me
literal-minded. But it's my only way of seeing the next
and the next familiar thing that raises itself out of anonymity.

Forgive me this invented ritual. Now, I'm watching
a kestrel con the field from fifty feet above. Minutes ago,

I noted its warm russet back, the stunning slate blue head
marked with black slashes. Lord, I'm more birdwatcher

than acolyte, this raptor's fierce attention waking me
to the rapture of looking, its tail and narrow wings
adjusting the sleek body in the invisible currents
until it comes to a hovering standstill, at rest on air.

**Four.**

# Beach Path

It's still there. So are my dead parents
in their bathing suits and white terrycloth robes,
trundling their beach bags, chairs, and umbrellas.

The path connects woods to river, connects
the shadowy light shouldering through
swamp maples to the river's bright, blinding light

where the path opens on a stretch of beach.
The river is there of course as well,
first, in its cadence against the banks

where old trees have given way to erosion,
and then in the honeyed color of clear water
over sand. Around the bend, the voices of children

still discovering turtles and dragonflies.
The water distills the late afternoon light
and the amber current keeps moving

late summer's first yellow leaves downriver.
In their chairs my parents watch the day slide by.
Sandpipers in flocks of five and six veer in

towards the beach, then away, and cliff swallows
meet their doubles in the river's mirroring surface.
When my parents gather up their things,

and leave once again on the beach path,
I stay by the river, listening to their voices fade
into a veery's cascade of downward spiraling notes.

# Dragonfly

*The devil's darning needle*, my father joked, *it sews up*
*the lips of boys who talk too much*—then smiled.

We're waiting for the sun to appear again
from behind the clouds and light the way down

the bronzy water, all the way to the sunken logs
where two or three larger bass, only a head or tail

appearing, disappearing in the sun, shadow,
cool themselves in the deeper water.

A dragonfly curls its tail on the boat's gunnel.
And here, now, on my patio in stop-motion.

It's resting on my bare leg.
Now that it's winged, its death is near.

My father is dead, I am sixty-seven.
That day, almost sixty years ago, he must have been

in his late twenties. I'd like to see his face more clearly.
Most likely we hardly exchanged a look,

caught up in the quiet, in the depths that kept changing
from sun into shadow, shadow into sun.

A breeze in the trees and then over water
silvers the leaves and then the water's mercurial surface.

In the shallows where the river turns gold over sand,
a gravid sunfish circles the perimeter of its scraped-out nest . . .

The dragonfly is still here on my leg.
Between us, there's a covenant.

I will not move; the dragonfly will remain, its blue-gold
wings alive with sunlight.

For as long as I can hold still, my father and I,
anchored in the river's pocket of sun and shade.

When the dragonfly flies into the blue sky
the needle its body makes

sews the seam shut between that darker water
and this bright sky.

# Outside the Door

*(Bonnard's "Dining Room in the Country")*

I am in Pierre Bonnard's dining room
in Vernonnet, and I don't want to leave.
It is commonplace and radiant.
The door fully open, both sides
of a casement window as well, light enters
like a neighbor, no need to knock, enlivening
the orange-red of the walls.
For an hour now I've been between worlds,
trying to figure why the blossoms outside
on a plum tree become the curtain's
pattern inside, or the curtain's pattern
the purple of the blossoms.
Even the door's threshold dissolves
into the colors of plum blossoms and curtains—
a step both into the outside
and into the colors of a girl's dress.

She is outside, though in the perspective
of the painting, she could be miles away.
Still, the opalescence of the opened door,
of the tablecloth and the cups and saucers
on the table, and even of a cat perched on a chair,
slide into one another, all leading to the girl,
barely visible, at the edge of a flowerbed
under a lustrous sky moving
toward sunset. Or is it sunrise?
And more—for no reason I can explain,
the girl, who truly is ghostlike, there and not there
depending on my angle of vision,
becomes my mother in an old photograph

I have of her as a girl. My mother,
dead now nearly two years, who has not
revisited me even in dream, is now
right outside the dining room where I am.

The girl seems exactly where she should be,
exactly where she needs to be,
even if Bonnard keeps me from knowing
where exactly that is. If I could speak to her,
she would answer in my mother's voice,
but she's sitting inside a magic circle
that no one, not even I, can enter,
even if some ongoing correspondence
seems to be taking place between
the pinkish-red dabs of color that compose
her face and the pinkish-blue color
of the flowers and the sky, and the purples
of the curtains that extend to
my mother's bluish-purple dress
and tip the blue-green mountains beyond her—
as if all these colors, so sensuous, so alive,
form a kind of unity, something like being
with my mother, but more shadowy,
a kind of peace from which I cannot get free.

# Ritual

Bent over my new grandson's crib,
I find myself again at thirty-four bent over
my newborn, now thirty, and I recall how,
called out of sleep, I'd rouse myself, listen,
then make my way in the dark to where
my new son lay. During those first unreal days
I needed to see in order to believe
my week-old child was breathing. Each night
I'd track his breath coming and going,
his tiny chest pulsing beneath my gentling hand.
The night sky wheeled above the house like the dream
I imagined wheeling in my child's dreaming head.
Lying there, eyes closed, then half-open,
he looked at me as if he were waiting to be recognized.
Or, still in the innocence of his birth, he had
something to tell me, though no way of saying
what it was he had already forgotten,
or still knew, but in a way that was entirely
without thought or words. I touched his shoulders
and face, counted and held his curled fingers
and weighed his legs in the palm of my hand.

That first week, the moon, its light diffused by fog,
moved weightlessly across the fields. Inside,
shadows chose the still clinging leaves of an oak,
or a chair or dresser and moved them without intention
or meaning across the floor and walls
of that rented house three thousand miles from home.
So many nights I'd sit there, fearful of everything to come
that I couldn't know; I listened, I watched,
trying to stay awake. Failing to. When my son's cries

announced him somewhere in my sightless sleep,
the stars were slipping away, and the colorless sky
seemed to be breathing itself into being,
and I woke, again and again as I needed to,
into the knowledge that my son was here, truly here.

# Courtesy

Even now, nearly fifty years later, the sound
of a basketball on pavement has me
back on Jimmy's driveway, Jimmy, Stan,
and Ed (dead now nearly all those years),
coming unsummoned out of their houses,
one of us, let's say it's me this time, suffering
some predictable teenage heartache,
dribbling a ball to give the after-school-
late-afternoon a cadence, the rhythm
of dribble, shoot, silence, and then the ball
again, clanging against the rim, bouncing
on the driveway. Together, no one says
a blessed word, not one of them says her name,
but they tender the ball to me more than usual,
and I catch and shoot, imitating Jerry West's
quick release, the ball caught at my chest
and lifted high over my head, one hand
steadying, the other following through,
arcing the ball towards the rim.
Soon the sighs I'm holding inside turn to grunts
as we go at it, two on two, and no one
seems to mind when I foul them too hard,
or take another foolish shot. The game
runs into the dark, the driveway light
turned on, all of us trash-talking one another,
the ball going up and in, our breath coming harder,
the shadows of our bodies on the garage door
like hieroglyphs telling a story
we couldn't possibly decipher, though I think now
it must have had something to do with that silence
we kept between us, that moved time along

until, at last, in the dark, we nodded to each other,
as if to say, *Hell, the day is over,*
*and tomorrow, tomorrow will be better.*

# Laundry

This morning, doing the laundry,
smoothing collars and shirt plackets
before placing it all in the dryer,
I saw the ghost of my recently dead mother,
her red-capillaried face looking on
approvingly in the steam.

I didn't expect to see her,
and some of this must be pretend,
but she *was* there, making a place for herself
over by the baskets, in the light
that fell through the windows
at an angle that never seemed to change.

We got to talking—who doesn't want
to talk with the dead again
when it's morning and mostly sunny?—
about our old backyard and the telephone pole
we planted there to carry the wash in
and out, its squeaking pulleys and ropes.

I was lingering over the way a drying sheet
took in a breeze and released it
as if it were breathing,
but my mother chattered away nonstop,
moving as she always did, from topic
to topic without transition,

only pausing here and there to punctuate
with one of her sayings—
*Doing the wash makes you happy.*
*It says you can begin again.*

And unlike when she was alive
that seemed true. As the light's angle

sharpened, none of our mistakes,
our fights or failures, the old
argument about dad—or even
the ridiculous, proper way
to fold a bottom sheet—held us back
as we finished the first load of darks.

And by the time she held a shirt
by the shoulders, folded it in thirds,
then flipped the bottom half under the top
and laid it in the pile for the living,
I was whistling, caught up entirely
in the rhythm and pace of our task.

# Kidnapped

Just now, by accident and without anything special
required on my part, I slipped out of history
and into, let's call it wonder,
my whole body applauding a madcap deer
triple-jumping a highway of cars,
then fitting its body between trees
perfectly situated for taking it in.

And sure, I'm all smiles for the deer
crossing unharmed and the random pattern of cars
that sped by without incident,
but now there's the aftereffect I can't account for—
the dizzying quick change of a blizzard
of falling leaves that becomes a flock of starlings,
a few hundred birds rising up
as if some signal had been given
and then, savants of air, turning as one bird
into a sky bluer than it was before.

Here I am driving, sitting up straight,
looking around as if I've been kidnapped
and my life depended on what I see.
And I can't believe what's here—
a car going by with three children wearing crowns
from Burger King; a stand
of expressive larches moving in the wind,
my finger on the wheel conducting
their adagio. Now the clouds require attention
and I see how they, too, go along with the wind
and the starlings, all of them moving together,
only themselves, and yet each of them
spilling beyond the boundaries
that keep them separate most days.

# Graveyard Prayer

Lord, here I am again at the graveyard where I'll be
buried, but for now where I rest before walking
back home. I like to lie with my back on the grass
and study the clouds, a Constable imposter,
or sit on my gravesite and look at this little village—
the cemetery, seven old houses facing south,
their western windows mirrors in the late light,
a small dam and waterfall that create a backyard lake,
and the little bridge over the outlet brook
that curves away to my right into the woods.
Yes, it's all too easy, the day still to be enjoyed
as it won't be when I'm steeping in my own juices.

It's fall appropriately, summer's green leaves following
their ordained paths to russet and gold. Lord, I don't come
to reflect. Perhaps I should. Late sixties, and my life,
at least up to now, and since turning thirty, has been
on a lucky streak. I'd call it grace, especially the gift
of lasting love I've had, but that seems too presumptuous.
Forgive me, but sitting here is just another chance to look
at what I'll be leaving behind. And if I've spent my life
trying to look at what I can't see by looking at what I can,
I've never much focused on what's to come, but only on
what's here, a kind of daily gift and daily leave-taking
and, I hope, a kind of practice for my end.

# After

Well, we're older now. Nothing new
there. We did and yet didn't know
from that very first *I do* how we'd follow
the years towards *who will bury who?*

So tell me again, when our lives are done,
that we'll be together. It's okay
if you lie to me. That's a price I'll pay
for our marriage to continue after we're gone.

Say it, please. Say how it will always be
when we meet again. After everything
we made together is torn apart, nothing
left of us but this paper wish. Tell me.

# Anniversary Gift

After reading that hummingbirds
are so light eight of them can be mailed
for the price of a first-class stamp,
I close my eyes and see them, fully revived,
rising out of some envelope of old memories.
I'll name them again as we once did
so long ago—Rufous, Anna's, and Broad-tailed—
darting to and from the feeders, sipping,
then retreating, flying jewels
the Spanish called them, and now I recall
how one of the Anna's, its garnet head
and throat glowing in the misted air,
hung like a jewel at your ear.

Here they are, or the memory of them.
Remember that trying-too-hard-to-be-hip
B&B in Telluride, a hot tub on the roof;
above the water, crisscrossing strings
decorated with Japanese lanterns
and four red heart-shaped feeders that brought
close the ebullience of the hummingbirds.
They surged around us, their kaleidoscope
of iridescent colors lightening
the cool, rainy day and helping us forget
the fogged-in, dim presence of the Rockies
we had come for and couldn't see.
Curtained in the tub's steaming air,
soon enough our eyes were in love
with birds we couldn't stop looking at,
their scintillant existence drawing
jeweled lines we swore we could see.

Which is why I'm bringing back the past,
those tiny birds disappearing
into all the years behind us now,
but today returning all at once,
as if some blessing had been conferred
without my asking; and so
I offer them to you, hoping these words,
even though they dim the colors as they must,
will draw for you their sweet transport.

# Notes

*Talking Turkey*: The poet I refer to is Galway Kinnell.
*Backyard Kingdom*: The poet I refer to is Ruth Stone.
*Source*: The poet I refer to is Billy Collins.
*Soleil & Sons*: The Herbert poem is "The Elixir." This poem is dedicated
   to Paul Harman, S.J.

# Acknowledgments

Grateful acknowledgment is made to the following journals, in which these poems were first published, sometimes in a slightly different version and with a different title:

*Anglican Theological Review*: "Sugar Maple"
*The Bellingham Review*: "Plenty," "Prayer with Dog and Rooster"
*The Common*: "Looking Up in the Backyard," "Obituary"
*The Georgia Review*: "Source," "Outside the Door"
*The Gettysburg Review*: "Kidnapped"
*Hampden-Sydney Review*: "Dragonfly," "Spring Again," "Room with Three Windows"
*Harvard Review Online*: "Talking Turkey"
*The Hudson Review*: "November"
*Ibbetson Street:* "Lake George"
*Image*: "Backyard Kingdom," "Graveyard Prayer," "Poverty," "Spring Begetting," "Morning Prayer with Hopkins' Kestrel"
*Kestrel*: "Little Did I Know"
*Mockingbird*: "My Neighbor's Mailbox"
*New Ohio Review*: "Prayer While Driving Home After My Yearly Physical," "Laundry," "Anniversary Gift"
*One*: "Aubade"
*Salamander*: "Beach Path," "Soleil & Sons"
*The Sewanee Review*: "Ritual," "Toast to My Dead Parents," "After," "Middle Tint"
*The Southern Poetry Review:* "Cedar Waxwings"
*The Southern Review*: "Courtesy," "Dock Life"
*Spiritus*: "Roadside Petition After March Snow Melt," "Remembering Debbie in Chimayo"

*Superstition Review*: "Weather Report to My Mother"
*Tar River Poetry*: "Supermoon"
*Terrain*: "Overtaken," "Roadside Homily"
*Worcester Poetry Review:* "Evening Prayer with Opening Question"
*Upstreet*: "Across the Water"

"Outside the Door," "Soleil & Sons," and "Supermoon" appeared on *Poetry Daily*'s website.

"Toast to My Dead Parents" appeared in *The Best American Poetry 2018*.

I'm especially grateful once again to Jeffrey Harrison and William Wenthe, whose attention and skill have made so many of these poems better.

# CavanKerry's Mission

CavanKerry Press is committed to expanding the reach of poetry to a general readership by publishing poets whose works explore the emotional and psychological landscapes of everyday life.

# Other Books in the Notable Voices Series

*Without My Asking* has been set in Acumin Pro, a neo-grotesque sans-serif typeface, intended for a balanced and rational quality. It was designed by Robert Slimbach for Adobe in 2015.